At the Dentist

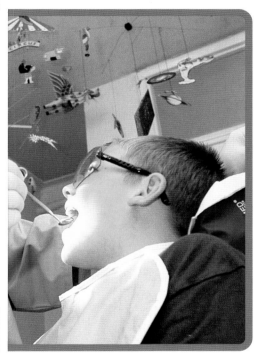

Chancellor

Photographs: Chris Fairclough

W
FRANKLIN WATTS
LONDON • SYDNEY

This edition 2006

First published in 2003 by
Franklin Watts
338 Euston Road
London
NW1 3BH

Franklin Watts Australia
Hachette Children's Books
Level 17/207 Kent Street
Sydney
NSW 2000

A CIP catalogue record for this book is available
from the British Library.

ISBN (10) 0 7496 6938 1
ISBN (13) 978-0-7496-6938-6
Dewey Classification Number 617.6

Series Editor: Jackie Hamley
Cover Design: Peter Scoulding
Design: Ian Thompson

Photos
All commissioned photographs by Chris Fairclough.
The publishers would like to thank the following
for permission to use photographs:

John Birdsall Photo Library 27 (bottom)

The author and publisher would especially like to thank everyone at Baigel,
Shah and Associates for giving their help and time so generously.

Printed in Malaysia

Contents

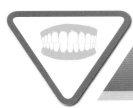

Meet the team

■ **Dentists help us look after our teeth and gums. The place where we go to see the dentist is called a dental surgery.**

These people work in a dental surgery in a town called Hoddesdon. They are a team and work together very closely.

1. Philip
2. Sujay
3. Vivek
4. Daphne
5. Jean
6. Jade
7. Sally
8. Jackie
9. Wendy

Philip, Sujay and Vivek are **dentists**.
Daphne, Jean and Jade are **dental nurses**.
Sally is a **dental hygienist**.
Wendy and Jackie are receptionists.

Dentists, hygienists and dental nurses wear special clothes at work. This is to help keep themselves and the surgery clean and **hygienic**.

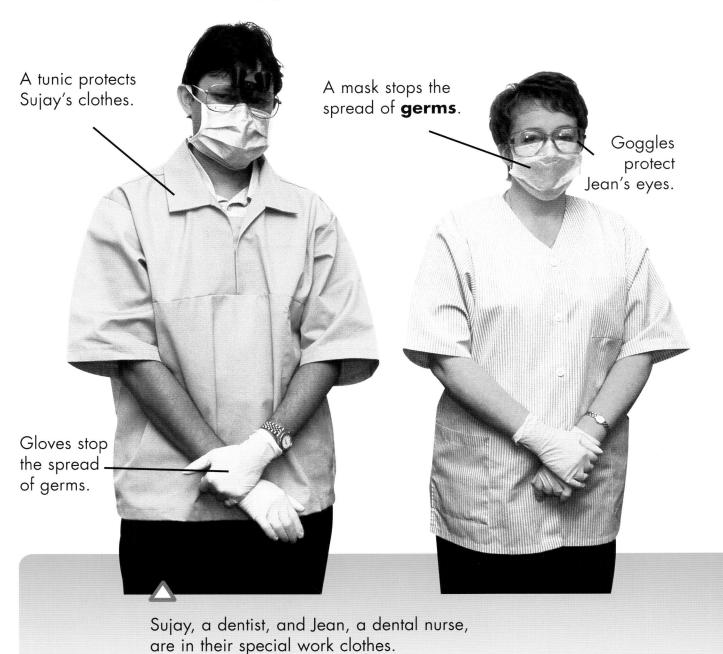

A tunic protects Sujay's clothes.

A mask stops the spread of **germs**.

Goggles protect Jean's eyes.

Gloves stop the spread of germs.

Sujay, a dentist, and Jean, a dental nurse, are in their special work clothes.

The dental surgery

▨ We go to a dental surgery for check-ups, and to have treatment on our teeth.

The dental surgery in Hoddesdon opens at 9 o'clock in the morning. Each dentist sees about twenty patients a day.

The dentists who work in the surgery have their names on brass plates outside the entrance.

SUJAY SHAH
B.D.S. (U.BIRM.)
DENTAL SURGEON

There are three dentists at our surgery. Between us, we have over ten thousand patients!
Philip, dentist

In the waiting room, a quiz game on the computer teaches patients how to look after their teeth.

When patients arrive at the surgery for an **appointment**, they first see the receptionist so she knows that they are there. Then they wait in the waiting room until the dentist can see them. While they wait, patients read magazines, watch television or play on a computer.

FACT

What to do if you need a dentist and the surgery is closed:

▷ Phone the surgery.

▷ Listen to the recorded message.

▷ Write down the telephone number of the dentist on duty.

▷ Phone the duty dentist and arrange an emergency appointment.

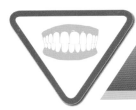

The reception

People have to book an appointment to see a dentist. Usually they phone up the reception to do this.

Wendy and Jackie are receptionists at the surgery. They answer the phones and write appointments in the diaries.

The receptionists also look after the patients' **dental records**. They keep the dental record cards in a filing cabinet.

Each dentist has a separate appointment diary, which is kept at the reception desk.

All the dental records kept in this cabinet are also stored on computer.

Wendy has just made an appointment for a patient. She writes to confirm the date and time. Patients may have to pay a fine if they miss an appointment.

Wendy writes out a reminder card to send to the patient at home.

Every day, the receptionists prepare an appointment list for each dentist. This list shows all the appointments for the following day. When the dentists arrive at work in the morning, they read their appointment lists to see which patients are coming in.

A receptionist puts the patients' dental records with the appointment list, so the dentist knows who the patients are and what their teeth are like.

New patients

▦ It is easy to become a new patient at a dental surgery.

Pete has just moved to Hoddesdon and needs to register with a dentist. He goes to the dental surgery and fills in a new patient form at the reception desk. He also arranges a check-up.

Jackie the receptionist arranges for Pete to have a check-up with Sujay, one of the dentists.

At Pete's first check-up, Sujay examines Pete's teeth. Jean, the dental nurse, makes notes on Pete's new dental record card.

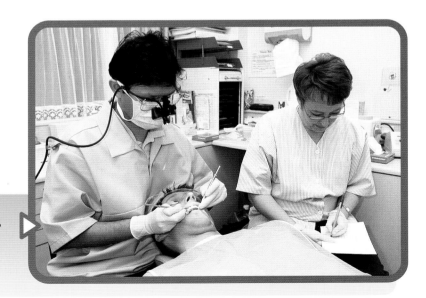

Sujay's goggles make things look bigger. They are called magnifying loupes.

Pete has an **x-ray**, to help Sujay examine his teeth in more detail. The x-ray is digital, so Pete and Sujay can look at it straight away on the computer screen.

It is easy to spot **tooth decay** on an x-ray.

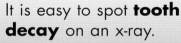

Pete doesn't need any treatment now. But Sujay shows him how to brush his teeth properly, to make sure they stay strong and healthy.

Sujay teaches his patients with a huge toothbrush and giant model teeth.

> *Don't forget to change your toothbrush every couple of months. Bent, worn-out bristles do not clean teeth very well!*
> **Sujay, dentist**

Having a check-up

Everyone should have regular check-ups with the dentist.

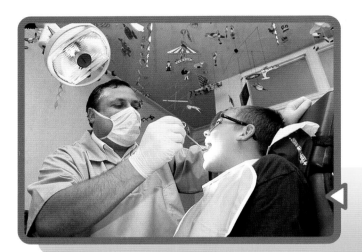

Dentists like to see their patients every six months. Andrew has come to see Philip for a check-up.

Philip tries to make his surgery bright and friendly, to help his patients relax.

FACT

▷ Children have 20 milk teeth.

▷ Milk teeth fall out from the age of five or six.

▷ Big teeth grow to replace the milk teeth.

▷ Adults have 32 big teeth.

Philip uses a tiny **intra-oral camera** to look inside Andrew's mouth.

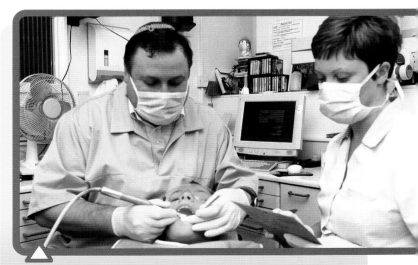

The tiny camera in Andrew's mouth shows a picture of the inside of his mouth.

As part of the check-up, Philip usually cleans the patient's teeth. This gets rid of **plaque** on the teeth.

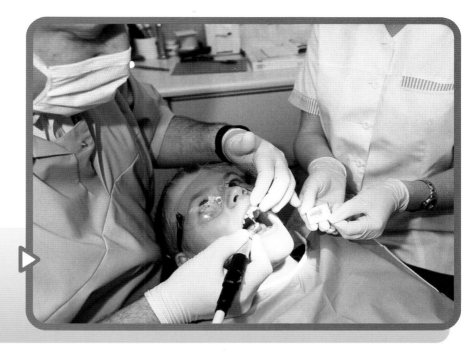

Jade the dental nurse hands Philip equipment to polish Andrew's teeth.

If patients are too old or sick to get to the dental surgery, dentists will visit them at home. Home visits usually happen after morning surgery.

Sujay is leaving the surgery to go on a home visit. He has got all the equipment he needs in his case.

The dental hygienist

Dental hygienists are experts at cleaning teeth. They also advise patients on how to keep their mouths healthy.

Pete has made an appointment to see Sally, the dental hygienist at the surgery.

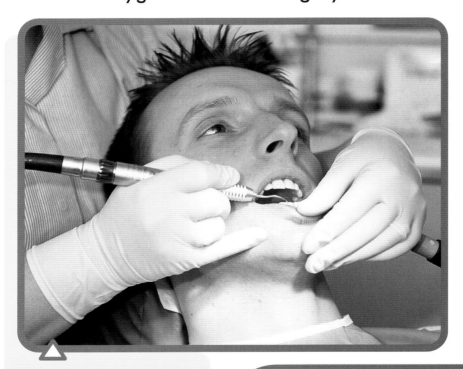

A suction tube sucks **saliva** and water out of Pete's mouth as Sally works.

Pete has some **tartar** on his teeth. Sally begins cleaning his teeth by removing the tartar with a machine called an ultrasonic scaler.

> *I teach lots of grown-ups how to clean their teeth properly. It is never too late to learn how to look after your teeth.*
>
> **Sally, dental hygienist**

Next Sally removes any stubborn stains from Pete's teeth using an air polishing machine. This machine blasts tiny bits of sand at the teeth and gets rid of stains quickly.

Sally then uses an electric brush with pink paste on it to give Pete's teeth a good polish.

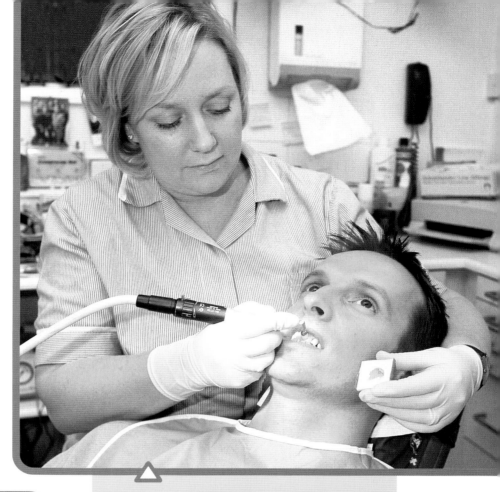

Sally's last job is to give Pete's teeth a final polish.

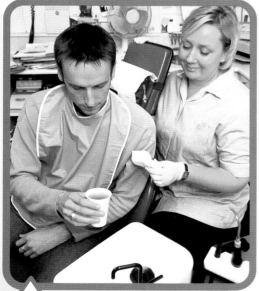

The antiseptic rinse kills germs and leaves a nice taste in your mouth!

When Sally has finished, Pete swills his mouth out with an **antiseptic** rinse. His teeth feel very clean now.

Sally ends by telling Pete to brush his teeth every morning and evening and not to eat too many sweets!

Dental treatment

■ **Sometimes people need to have dental treatment. A separate appointment is usually made for this.**

Freddie has arrived at reception with his mum. He has an appointment to have a **filling**, because one of his teeth has a small **cavity**.

Jackie tells Freddie to go to Philip's surgery.

Philip uses a water drill to clean out the decayed part in Freddie's tooth. This leaves a small hole in the tooth. Philip will put the filling into the hole.

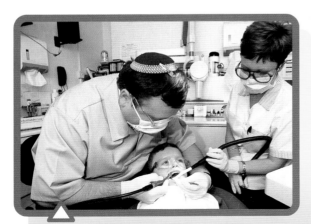

Philip, Jade and Freddie are wearing goggles to protect their eyes.

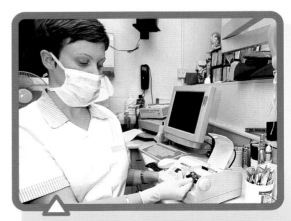

Jade mixes up white filling material in a machine. This takes about ten seconds.

Philip squirts the filling mixture into the hole in Freddie's tooth. He then uses a light cure machine to set the filling. The bright blue light on the light cure machine quickly hardens the filling.

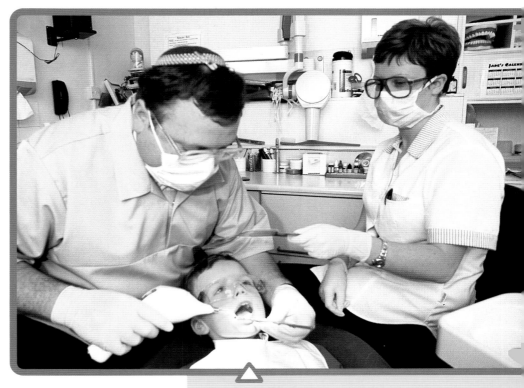

Jade holds up a pink filter to protect everyone's eyes from the bright light.

Freddie is lucky. The cavity in his tooth has been treated quickly so that the decay did not get any worse. If teeth are left to rot, they start to hurt. In the end, it might be impossible to treat them and the teeth might even have to be taken out.

Freddie is given a sticker and a balloon for being a good patient.

Emergency!

In an emergency, patients need to see a dentist straight away. There is no time to wait for an appointment.

Natalie has fallen off her bike and knocked out one of her teeth. She has rushed to the dental surgery with her mum and sister.

SHAH & ASSOCS
AL PRACTICE
EN Mon. - Fri.
00am - 5.45pm
rly Closure On Friday Afternoons.
te Night - 8pm Wed
2.30 - 1.30 (reception o

Natalie's sister holds the tooth in a glass of milk. This is the best way to preserve it.

Vivek looks in Natalie's mouth to see the damage caused by the accident. He gives Natalie an injection so that she won't feel any pain.

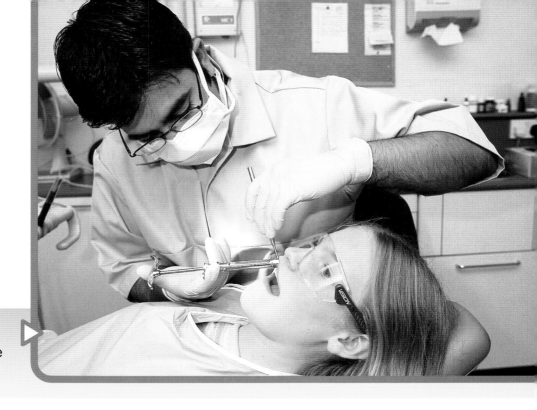

Vivek acts quickly and calmly. Natalie is very brave.

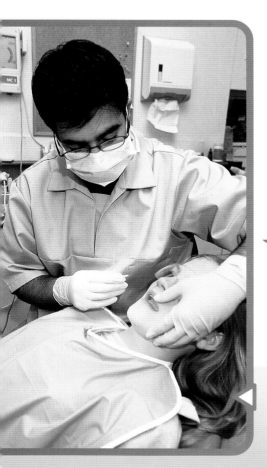

Patients often have accidents in the playground, or when playing on bikes. If a tooth is knocked out, put it in milk or water and go to see your dentist as quickly as you can.
Vivek, dentist

Natalie's tooth is still in one piece, so Vivek is able to put it back into her mouth. Emergency cases like Natalie's need to be treated within one hour of the accident for the mouth to heal.

Natalie's tooth will soon tighten up in her gum and her mouth will heal.

Dental equipment

⊞ Dentists need lots of equipment. Some instruments are modern, but others have been used for many years.

Some old dental instruments, such as the dental mirror, are worked by hand.

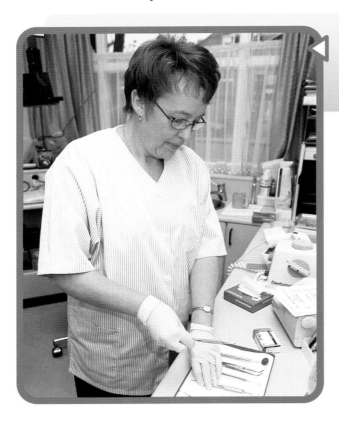

Jean the dental nurse lays out some manual instruments for a dentist to use.

Many modern instruments, such as the ultrasonic scaler and air polisher, are operated by machine.

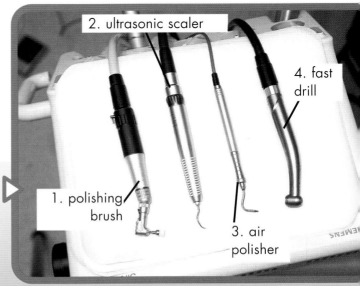

2. ultrasonic scaler

4. fast drill

1. polishing brush

3. air polisher

1. The polishing brush polishes teeth.
2. The ultrasonic scaler removes tartar.
3. The air polisher shoots air and tiny grains of sand to blast away stains.
4. The fast drill cleans out decay.

A **compressor** supplies the power for machine-operated equipment. The compressor is kept in the basement. A suction machine is also kept there. This provides the suction power for the machines that remove saliva from the patient's mouth.

The suction machine is kept with the compressor in the basement.

Some dental equipment, including the digital x-ray machine, is computerised.

FACT

▷ All the machines in the surgery are checked regularly.

▷ Maintenance experts come into the surgery to service the machines.

▷ Most machines are serviced once a year.

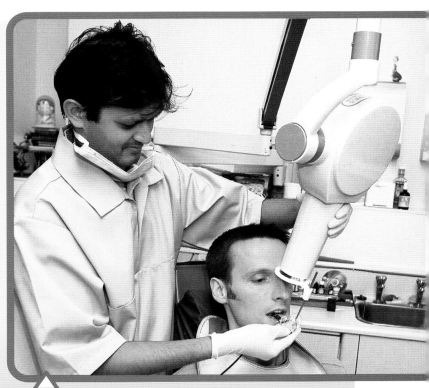

Digital x-rays are very useful as they allow the dentist to see what is happening inside the teeth and gums.

Cleaning up!

▦ It is very important to keep the dental surgery clean and hygienic, so it is free of germs.

In the evening, cleaners come in to the surgery. They make sure all the rooms are spotless and ready for the next day. The dental nurses also work hard to keep the surgery free of germs.

Dental nurses use a machine called a **steriliser** to clean equipment. They put used equipment on a metal tray, which goes in the steriliser.

Dental nurses clean as much as they can during the day.

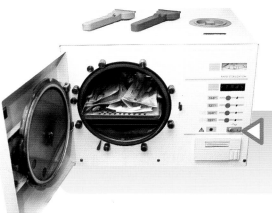

In the steriliser, the equipment is cleaned with pressurised steam. The high temperature of the steam (134°C) kills germs.

Dental equipment must be kept free of germs.

When dentists have finished using a piece of equipment, they put it in sterilising liquid until it can be cleaned in the steriliser.

Some dental equipment is disposable. This means it can only be used once, then it is thrown away.

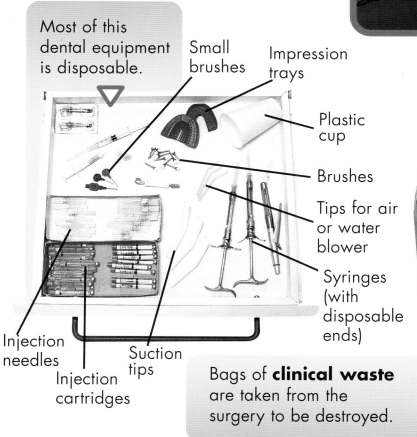

Most of this dental equipment is disposable.

Small brushes

Impression trays

Plastic cup

Brushes

Tips for air or water blower

Syringes (with disposable ends)

Injection needles

Injection cartridges

Suction tips

Bags of **clinical waste** are taken from the surgery to be destroyed.

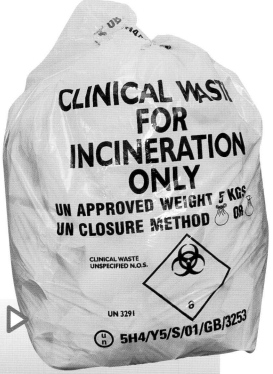

CLINICAL WASTE FOR INCINERATION ONLY

UN APPROVED WEIGHT 5 KGS OR

UN CLOSURE METHOD

CLINICAL WASTE UNSPECIFIED N.O.S.

UN 3291

5H4/Y5/S/01/GB/3253

Orthodontics

Orthodontics is a type of dental treatment that helps crooked teeth grow straight. This treatment may take quite a long time.

Sometimes a patient's teeth are too close together. This is called overcrowding. Overcrowded teeth can be helped with a **brace.**

Delroy is a **dental technician**. He works in a laboratory to make braces. He also makes other things for dental patients, such as crowns. Crowns cover and protect teeth if they have been broken.

Delroy has come into the surgery to show Sujay a brace he has made.

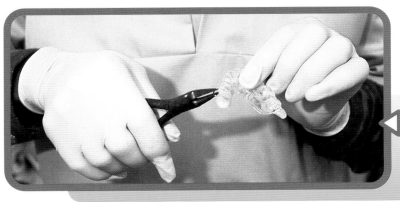

The brace may need to be adjusted to fit the patient.

When dentists check children's teeth, they usually look for overcrowding. It is best to begin to treat orthodontic problems at a young age, if possible.

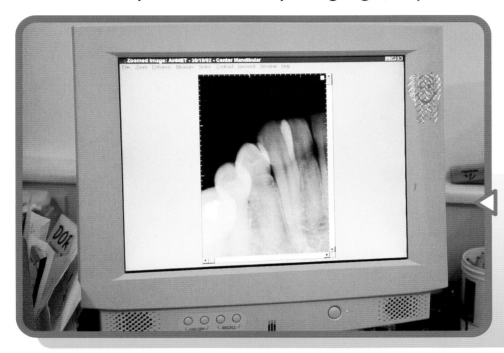

This x-ray shows overcrowded teeth in a child's mouth. This child needs to see an **orthodontist** for treatment.

Sally is wearing a "train track" brace. The brace is fixed onto her teeth and slowly works to bring the teeth in line with each other. She will have to wear it for about two years.

When the brace is finally taken off, Sally will have a perfect smile!

Looking after your teeth

Tooth decay is the main reason why people get toothache. You can prevent tooth decay by following these simple steps:

1. Only have sugary foods and drinks at mealtimes.

2. Don't eat sugary snacks between meals. The more often you have sugary food and drink, the more likely you are to get tooth decay.

3. If you have to eat a snack, stick to cheese, vegetables or fresh fruit.

4. DON'T FORGET TO BRUSH YOUR TEETH! Always brush your teeth in the morning and before you go to bed.

HOW TO CLEAN YOUR TEETH

1. Choose a toothbrush with a small head and soft, nylon bristles.

2. Don't put too much toothpaste on the brush. A pea-sized blob is enough.

3. Brush your teeth in small, circular movements.

4. Don't forget to brush behind your teeth and onto your gums.

5. Make sure you brush all your teeth, right to the back of your mouth.

6. Don't rush when you brush; it should take about three minutes to clean your teeth properly.

7. Make sure your toothbrush is in good condition. When it wears out, get a new one.

Glossary

antiseptic A substance that kills germs.

appointment An arrangement to visit somebody, for example a dentist, at a particular time.

brace A piece of dental equipment made to move teeth into the right position.

cavity A decayed part in a tooth that causes a hole.

clinical waste Used equipment that needs to be thrown away. Clinical waste must be disposed of carefully.

compressor A machine that uses air pressure as a source of power for the machine-operated equipment.

dental hygienist Someone who is trained to clean teeth and help people with their dental health.

dental nurse Someone who is trained to support the dentist in the dental surgery.

dental record Notes which contain details of a patient's teeth and any dental treatment they have had.

dental technician Someone who makes dental appliances, for example braces, crowns and false teeth.

dentist Someone who is trained to look after people's teeth and gums.

filling A small piece of material put inside a tooth cavity to replace a decayed part of the tooth.

germs Tiny living organisms that can cause disease.

hygienic Clean and free of germs.

intra-oral camera A tiny camera used to see clearly inside the mouth.

orthodontics A type of dental treatment that corrects crooked teeth.

orthodontist A dentist who specialises in orthodontics.

plaque A soft layer which forms on teeth in between brushing. Plaque is full of harmful bacteria, which can cause tooth decay and gum disease.

saliva The natural liquid, or spit, in a person's mouth.

steriliser A machine which uses pressurised hot steam to clean equipment. The heat kills all germs.

tartar Plaque that has not been removed and has become hard. Tartar cannot be removed by brushing and needs to be scraped off.

tooth decay When teeth rot because plaque has mixed with sugar.

x-ray A photograph that shows bones etc. underneath the skin. Dentists use x-rays to see what is happening inside teeth and gums.

Further information

To find out more about dentists and how to look after your teeth, you could visit:

www.dentalhealth.org.uk

To find out more about dentistry in Australia, visit:

www.ada.org.au

Note to parents and teachers: Every effort has been made by the Publishers to ensure that these websites are suitable for children; that they are of the highest educational value, and that they contain no inappropriate or offensive material. However, because of the nature of the Internet, it is impossible to guarantee that the contents of these sites will not be altered. We strongly advise that Internet access is supervised by a responsible adult.

The British Dental Health Foundation is a charity that helps people learn about oral and dental health. For more information, write to the Foundation at this address:

British Dental Health Foundation
Smile House
2 East Union Street
Rugby CV22 6AJ

or telephone: 0870 770 4000

The Foundation also runs a helpline for dental advice:

0845 063 11 88

Index